B-day Box

Haydn Middleton
Illustrated by Mark Weber

A Harcourt Achieve Imprint

www.Rigby.com
1-800-531-5015

Literacy by Design Leveled Readers: *The B-day Box*

ISBN-13: 978-1-4189-3924-3
ISBN-10: 1-4189-3924-2

© 2008 Harcourt Achieve Inc.

All rights reserved. No part of the material protected by this copyright may be reproduced or utilized in any form or by any means, in whole or in part, without permission in writing from the copyright owner. Requests for permission should be mailed to: Paralegal Department, 6277 Sea Harbor Drive, Orlando, FL 32887.

Rigby is a trademark of Harcourt Achieve Inc.

Printed in China
3 4 5 6 7 8 985 14 13 12 11 10 09 08

Contents

Chapter 1
The 11th Photograph 5

Chapter 2
Sleepover Scares .12

Chapter 3
Computer Creepiness 18

Chapter 4
A Second Warning 29

Chapter 5
Happy B-day to Me 35

Chapter 6
Grandma's Tale 39

Chapter 7
The Horrible Event 48

Chapter 8
Nadira's Worst Nightmare 55

Chapter 9
The B-day Box 60

Chapter 1
The 11th Photograph

Nadira Bakshi was so tired that she could barely keep her eyes open. Across the room her best friend, Alexis, was yawning wide enough to swallow the moon. It was Friday night, and Alexis was spending the night at Nadira's house. After hours of movies, popcorn, and talking, the two girls were completely exhausted.

The living room was theirs for the night. They were each buried under their blankets and pillows on the floor. All the lamps were turned off, and the soft glow of the TV lit the room, but it also cast strange and spooky shadows on the walls.

Both girls had promised each other that they'd try to stay up until midnight, just to see if they could. There was over an hour to go, and the chances of their actually being awake when 12 o'clock rolled around looked to be pretty slim.

Nadira's Doberman pinscher, Wolfgang, was already fast asleep. He was curled up in his bed on the floor next to Nadira so she could reach over and scratch him behind his ears. She liked sleeping with Wolfgang close by.

Nadira glanced over at her friend and saw that Alexis's eyes were completely closed. "You awake, Alexis?" she asked, throwing a pillow at her.

"What?" Alexis shot straight up. "I'm awake." She tossed Nadira's pillow back to her.

"We still have an hour to go. Don't fall asleep on me now."

"I'm not," Alexis yawned, stretching her arms up into the air.

"If we're going to make it, we need to do something besides watch TV."

"Well, we can't play video games," Alexis said. "They're too loud. The last thing we want is to wake up your parents."

Nadira snapped her fingers. "I know! You stay here. I'll be right back."

As silently as possible, Nadira snuck up the stairs, stopping every time the floor creaked. Luckily, the door to her parents' bedroom stayed closed. She crept to her room, then returned downstairs a minute later carrying one of her most prized possessions.

"Cool. What is that?" Alexis asked as Nadira sat cross-legged on the floor.

Nadira set a beautifully decorated wooden box down between them. It was red with yellow and gold painted swirls and flowers. A metal latch on the front kept the lid locked.

"This is my Birthday Box. I call it my B-day Box for short," Nadira said, taking out a small, metal key from a chain around her neck. She always kept the key with her so she'd always know where it was. "And I keep the box locked so my brother Naveen can't get into it."

"It's super neat," Alexis said.

"My grandmother gave it to me. It's from India. She goes back every few years to see our family there. On her last visit, she bought this box for me at a street market."

"What's in it?" Alexis asked, knocking on the top.

Nadira slipped the key inside the lock, gave it a turn, then opened the lid. The box was filled with keepsakes. A collection of old birthday cards was rubber-banded together. There was a stack of photographs, candles from birthday cakes, some purple and green ribbon, a dark-red cone hat, and some party noisemakers. Nadira blew softly into a noisemaker, just enough to make a quiet *blrrrrr*. Both girls giggled.

"My most favorite day of the whole year is my birthday," Nadira said. "I like to keep souvenirs from my birthday parties. It's sort of a time capsule. I unlock my B-day Box every year around my birthday and think about how much I've changed over the last 12 months."

"And your next birthday is on Sunday.

That's only two days away!"

Nadira nodded. "I'll be 11 years old."

"Wow. I haven't kept anything from any of my birthday parties." Alexis flipped through the treasures in the B-day Box. "What are those pictures?"

"These are the coolest things of all," Nadira said, taking the photographs out of the box. "They're family pictures taken every year on my birthday." She held one out to her friend. "See? This one was taken just last year, but this one was taken ten years ago when I was only one year old."

"It's the same people in both pictures," Alexis pointed out.

"It's always the same people," Nadira laughed. "Every year my grandpa takes the shot, and it always shows Naveen, Dad, me, Mom, and Grandma standing in front of the fireplace. Oh, and of course the most important member of our family, Wolfgang."

Alexis held up one of the older pictures. "Wolfgang's only a puppy in this one."

"He was my birthday present when I

was one year old. So on Sunday when I turn 11, he'll turn 10. We have the same birthday, don't we, boy?" Nadira reached over and scratched behind Wolfgang's ears. The dog cracked open an eye, stretched out his huge paws, then curled back up and was soon fast asleep.

As Alexis glanced down into the B-day Box, she twisted her mouth in confusion, as though she saw something that didn't belong. "Hey, Nadira, I think you forgot one of the pictures."

"I did?"

Nadira looked at where Alexis was

pointing. It was strange, but there was another picture in the box, tucked between a ribbon and some old wrapping paper. She counted the pictures in her hand. There were ten. She'd had ten birthdays. So what was this 11th photograph?

Hands shaking, Nadira picked up the photograph. It felt slightly different from all the others. It was colder to the touch, with thick, sharp edges. When she raised it to her face to get a better look, it smelled odd, too. It reminded her of the chemicals used to clean a swimming pool, only much, much stronger.

"Well?" Alexis asked. She sounded out of breath, like she'd just run a race. "What is it a picture of?"

Nadira swallowed hard, then said, "It's my birthday."

"But you already have ten birthday pictures here."

"I know," Nadira said. "It's a picture of my 11th birthday!"

Just then, the girls heard a soft click, and the TV went black.

Chapter 2
Sleepover Scares

The TV had been the only source of light in the dark living room, and now without it, the room was pitch black.

Nadira gasped. Terrified, Alexis grabbed Nadira's arm and squeezed much harder than she'd meant to. Wolfgang had risen from his bed and was standing protectively beside Nadira, growling.

There was a creak on the stairs, then another. The footsteps were heavy with the sound of thick-soled shoes. Someone was coming toward them. A dark figure could be seen on the bottom step. Nadira saw something in his hand.

A wicked laugh rocked the night. *Ha ha ha ha ha ha!*

Nadira screamed.

Alexis screamed.

Wolfgang barked.

The dark figure laughed again. *Ha ha ha ha ha!*

Just then, the door to Nadira's parents' bedroom opened, and out came her mom and dad in bathrobe and slippers, rubbing their eyes.

Nadira's mother, Sonali, flicked on the lights, while her father, Anupam, yawned. "What's going on down there?" he asked, a sleepy hand covering his mouth.

Alexis quickly reached over and flicked on the lamp. Standing at the bottom of the stairs, face and hands done up like a monster with claws, was Nadira's older brother Naveen. He had a foolish grin on his face.

"Boo!" Naveen cried, then started laughing uncontrollably. In his hand was the remote control he'd used to turn off the TV and scare the girls. Wolfgang trotted over to him and licked his hand, signaling that everything was OK.

"Naveen!" Nadira cried. "You scared us to death!"

This only made Naveen laugh more. In fact, he was still laughing as he walked back upstairs to his room. A few more laughs could be heard from behind his closed bedroom door.

Sonali came down the stairs. She had given her son a stern look as he'd passed, but now she was having a hard time trying not to smile.

"Shouldn't you girls be asleep by now?" she asked. "Lights out was over an hour ago."

"Sorry, Mrs. Bakshi," Alexis said, worried that she and Nadira were now not only terrified, but also in trouble. She scrambled back to her part of the floor and dove under the covers, completely covering her head. "We are going to sleep right now."

"That was mean of Naveen," Nadira told her mother.

"Yes, it was, honey," Sonali said. She reached for the lamp switch and flicked the lamp off. "But you have to admit that it was also a bit funny."

"I don't think so," Nadira protested.

"Sweet dreams, girls," Sonali said.

"Goodnight, Mrs. Bakshi!" came Alexis's muffled shout from beneath her mountain of blankets. For some reason Alexis always seemed shy around Nadira's mother.

The minutes ticked by, and slowly the house was quiet again. Before, the girls had fought to stay awake, but now neither of them could sleep. Wolfgang, on the other hand, had no trouble falling fast asleep. He'd gotten a big drink of water from his water dish and then went right back to bed. Nadira had given him a big hug for being such a good watchdog.

Finally, Alexis loudly whispered, "Nadira? Psst, Nadira! You asleep?"

"No," Nadira whispered back, just as loudly. "Are you?"

"No." There was a brief silence, then Alexis asked, "What did you do with that 11th picture? I never got a good look at it."

"It's here in my B-day Box, but it's too dark to see it. We can't turn on the lamp or my parents will wake up again."

Alexis crawled over. "I have a small flashlight here in my pillowcase."

"Why do you have a flashlight in your pillowcase?" Nadira asked.

Alexis shrugged. "Just because."

She pressed a button on the flashlight, and bright light shone up onto her face. Nadira thought the light made her friend look even scarier than her brother standing in the dark, but she didn't tell Alexis that. Instead, she took the mysterious 11th photograph out of the B-day Box, and together the two girls finally got a good look at it.

Just like in the other ten photos, Nadira's family stood in their usual positions. Naveen stood to the left, followed by her father Anupam, then Nadira herself in the middle, then her mother Sonali, and finally Nadira's grandmother. Everyone in the group was dressed up in their nice clothes, which was also part of the tradition. However, in this picture everyone had a grim, almost frightened look on their face—but no one had *ever* looked that way in the other birthday photos. It was as though some horrible event was happening right as the picture was being taken.

Nadira herself looked as though she might be screaming at something. She was dressed in a lovely red and yellow *sari* with a purple wrap around her middle. The sari was the traditional clothing an Indian woman wears, and this sari was one that she'd never seen before.

Just then, Alexis gasped. "Nadira! Do you see it?"

"See what?"

"That's just it! See *nothing*. There's nothing to see!"

And with those words, the whole truth suddenly dawned on Nadira. Looking down at all those unhappy faces in the photograph, she knew exactly what Alexis meant. This wasn't just a matter of what was in the picture, but of what *wasn't* in it—or rather, *who* wasn't.

There was an empty space in the photograph where her dog Wolfgang was supposed to be.

Chapter 3
Computer Creepiness

The next morning after Alexis had gone home from their sleepover, Nadira was determined to figure out the mystery of the strange photograph.

She was sure that there was a simple explanation for how the picture had gotten into her B-day Box. After all, it had been almost midnight when she and Alexis found the photograph. They were both pretty tired. But the 11th photograph was still there in the B-day Box the next morning, plain as day. The picture did exist. It wasn't a dream or sleepiness.

Maybe someone had put it there? That had to be it, she decided. Strange pictures didn't just appear on their own out of thin air.

Nadira would find out what her family knew, or if they could help. She'd show the picture to each of them and see if anyone knew where it had come from.

Nadira's father was a professional musician, which meant that he made a living writing and playing music. She found him in their basement, practicing his violin.

When the Bakshi family moved into this house, Anupam had turned the basement into his own personal practice room. There was special foam padding covering the walls that absorbed sound and kept it inside the room. That way, he could practice without disturbing his family upstairs—not that his playing ever disturbed Nadira. She loved to hear him play the violin. Her favorite was *The Magic Flute*, an opera by the Austrian composer Wolfgang Amadeus Mozart that was written in 1791.

Nadira knocked on the basement door. She could hear the soft sounds of violin music, so she knew he was in the middle of practice. Anupam was always glad to have Nadira sit with him as he played, so she knew it was OK to go and listen. She quietly slipped through the door and down the steps.

Anupam smiled as Nadira took a seat against the far wall. His playing was almost magical to her, like she could see the notes floating through the air. When he played something slow and sad, Nadira felt sad. When the song was fast and happy, Nadira smiled and tapped her foot.

And when her father had finished the song, Nadira clapped.

Anupam stood and bowed. "Thank you, sweetheart. I composed that myself."

"Really? You wrote that music? I think it's beautiful."

Pages of sheet music were spread out on the table in front of Anupam. He took his pencil and made some marks on the pages, hummed the tune to himself, then erased what he'd marked and wrote in new notes.

"Can I ask you something, Dad?"

"Sure, sweetheart," Anupam replied, flipping through the pages of sheet music. He put the pencil between his teeth, scratching his head in concentration.

"I found something strange in my B-day Box, something that wasn't supposed to be there."

Anupam stared off into space, humming a string of notes to himself. "That's great, sweetheart," he said, thinking about his music and not what she'd said.

Nadira knew that she'd better get his attention while she still could. "You know the photographs of all my past birthdays? There should only be ten, right? Last night, Alexis and I found an extra photograph. I think it's from my 11th birthday, and I haven't even had my 11th birthday yet!"

As Anupam made some marks on his sheet music, he said, "Your birthday isn't until tomorrow, sweetheart."

"I know, Dad. That's what makes it so scary."

Nadira's father hummed to himself, shook his head, hummed a different set of notes, then nodded. He made some more marks on the pages. "That's great, sweetheart."

"Great? It's not great, Dad." Nadira held out the picture to him. "See? I have it right here. This picture is *from the future*!"

Anupam glanced up from his work only for a second. He squinted at the photograph in Nadira's hand, then asked, "Did your brother make that on the computer?"

Nadira went back upstairs, leaving her father to his music. She'd try her mom next.

She found Sonali up in her bedroom, rushing between the closet and the dresser, getting dressed. Sonali zipped back and forth, throwing on a piece of clothing here, a necklace there, then her watch—she must have been running late.

Sonali was a real estate agent. She loved helping people buy and sell houses. And even though it was Saturday, she was getting dressed in her best suit. She'd be showing a house today to people who might want to buy it. And so Sonali had to look her best.

"You look really nice, Mom."

"Thanks, honey. Will you hand me those earrings?"

Nadira handed her mother a pair of silver earrings with green jewels in them. These were her mother's "lucky" earrings, which meant that this was an important house she was trying to sell. As Sonali put the earrings into her ears, she checked herself out in the bathroom mirror.

"Mom, I need to tell you something. It's about my B-day Box."

Sonali stared into the mirror as she brushed out her hair one final time. "Sure, honey. What's on your mind?" Then she glanced down at her watch. "Let's walk and talk, OK? I'm running a bit late."

"I found something strange," Nadira said as she chased her mother down the stairs and into her home office. "Something that wasn't supposed to be there."

"Oh really? That's great, honey," Sonali replied as she started shoveling papers into her briefcase.

"I found a picture from the future. It's from my 11th birthday."

Sonali stapled a stack of papers together, then shoved them inside her briefcase. She glanced hurriedly around the room as though she'd forgotten something. "Your birthday's not until tomorrow, honey. It's too early to start setting up for the party."

"I know, that's why this picture is from the future. But what's scary is that Wolfgang's not in it. I'm worried that something might happen to him."

Sonali checked the drawers of her desk, then found what she'd been looking for—her lucky pen. She tucked it inside her jacket. "Wolfgang, huh? That's great, honey."

"Great? It's not great," Nadira held the picture out for her mother. "See? Wolfgang's missing."

Sonali glanced at her daughter for only a second before an amused smile appeared on her face. She kissed Nadira on the forehead before heading toward the door.

"Did your brother make that on the computer?" she asked.

Was this all just another one of her older brother's mean jokes? Of course it was! Naveen must have scanned one of her old birthday pictures into his computer, made some changes, then printed out a new picture. But how could he have gotten into her B-day Box to get one of her old photographs when she always kept it locked?

It was time to find out some answers.

There was a yellow "KEEP OUT" sign on the door to Naveen's bedroom. Ignoring it, she knocked as loud as she could.

"Read the sign," her brother shouted from inside the room.

Nadira burst through the door. Naveen was sitting at his desk, feet up by his computer, with huge headphones covering his ears. His head nodded in time with the music he was listening to.

"You didn't read the sign," Naveen said.

"I need to talk to you. Have you been in my room lately? I found something weird in my B-day Box."

Naveen nodded.

"You have? Were you in my B-day Box? It's small and red, and I keep all my old birthday things inside."

Naveen nodded.

Nadira breathed a huge sigh of relief. She wasn't even mad that her brother had been in her room without permission. She was just glad that the 11th photograph was a fake.

"But how did you get into the box without the key?" Nadira asked, suddenly worried. "I always keep it on a chain around my neck."

Naveen nodded.

"How'd you do it?"

Naveen nodded.

"Naveen?"

Her brother had been watching her the whole time she'd been speaking, but now she saw that he hadn't heard a word she'd said.

"What?" he shouted, nodding his head in time with the music. "I didn't hear a word you said—the music's too loud."

Nadira sighed in frustration. She held the photograph out for her brother to see. He glanced at it, took it from her, then looked at it very closely. Nadira wouldn't even be mad at him for ignoring her when she was standing right there in front of him, if only he'd just see that this horrible photograph was from the future. Someone in her family had to believe her!

Naveen looked at the picture for another minute, then asked angrily, "Hey! Did you make this on my computer?"

Chapter 4
A Second Warning

Since her brother had proven to be no help at all, Nadira took the photograph and left his room. It was clear that no one in her family knew anything about the 11th photograph. There was no other explanation except that the picture was real and that it had mysteriously appeared out of thin air. And if the picture meant that Wolfgang was in some kind of danger, then the best thing would be for her to keep a close eye on him.

But where was he?

He wasn't in her room or in her parents' room. She searched downstairs, but there was no sign of him by his food dish or in his bed. She stuck her head out the back door, but he wasn't out in the yard either.

Then she spotted a furry little figure tucked away in the corner behind the couch. Wolfgang had chosen a very strange place for a nap, Nadira thought. This wasn't like him at all.

There was something out of place with him, something not quite right, but she couldn't think of what it was.

She scratched him behind his ears, then she tried to wake him up. Wolfgang cracked open an eye, but he wouldn't move. It took a minute or two of shaking before he finally stood. He walked slowly to his water dish in the kitchen, took a very big drink, then walked to his bed. He was asleep again in no time.

"You are turning into a very lazy dog," Nadira said.

As Wolfgang lay in his bed, she realized what it was that was out of place—for some reason his collar was missing.

Upstairs in her bedroom, Nadira sat on her bed, staring down at the photograph that had started this whole mess. The smell of swimming pool chemicals was still very strong. The picture felt cool in her hands, as though it had just come out of the refrigerator. She thought that if she weren't careful, she might cut herself on one of the sharp edges.

Nadira decided that she didn't want to think about this photograph or this mystery any more.

She went to her B-day Box sitting on top of her dresser, took the small key from around her neck, and unlocked the box.

But as she tossed the photograph inside, she saw something that sent a chill up her spine. She gasped and backed away several steps.

For the second time, she had found something in the box that wasn't supposed to be there.

With a trembling hand, she reached inside and pulled out Wolfgang's dog collar.

Not only that, the collar was dripping wet with water.

Nadira immediately called Alexis on the phone, and her friend rode her bike right over.

"OK, so tell me again what it was you saw," Alexis said as Nadira dragged her upstairs. "Wolfgang's water bowl was inside your B-day Box? How'd it fit?"

"Not his water bowl, his dog collar! And it was wet, just like the time it had slipped off his neck and I found it sitting in his water bowl."

"That's cool and creepy," Alexis smiled.

"No, it's not!" Nadira protested. "Something strange is going on."

"Well, you have to admit that it's sort of cool."

The girls found Wolfgang's collar on the floor in front of the dresser, right where Nadira had dropped it when she had run for the phone. Alexis went right to it and picked it up, but Nadira wasn't sure she wanted to touch it.

"It's dry," Alexis said.

"It is?" Nadira was beyond confused. "But it wasn't! It was dripping wet!"

Alexis studied the collar. "I think maybe it's a clue. There's the collar, and your dog is missing in the 11th photograph—both things point to Wolfgang." She thought hard for a minute. "Maybe it's a warning."

"A warning? From who?"

"I don't know. The box?"

Nadira snapped her fingers. "Of course! I've spent all this time focused on the 11th photograph when I should have been finding out more about the B-day Box."

"You got that box from your grandmother, right?" Alexis said. "Maybe we should ask her if she knows anything about what's been going on."

"She and my grandfather are coming into town tomorrow for my birthday party. We can ask her then." Nadira paused for a moment. "You are still coming, right?"

Alexis rubbed her chin thoughtfully. "Let's see, you're going to tell your grandmother that the mysterious box she bought you in India takes pictures of the future and stole your dog's collar when you weren't looking—I wouldn't miss it for the world!"

Chapter 5
Happy B-day to Me

Nadira woke the next morning, and she was one year older.

"Happy B-day to me," she said as she stretched. She smiled at the thought of the party and the birthday presents that awaited her that day. There would be 11 candles on her cake, and after blowing them all out in one breath, she'd eat as much as she could.

Then she rolled over, saw the B-day Box sitting on her dresser, groaned, and threw the blankets up over her head.

The house was quiet, too quiet it seemed. She'd slept late that Sunday morning, and usually her parents were up and going by now. Naveen always slept until noon, but Nadira expected her parents to be up by now.

Nadira crawled out of bed and tiptoed out into the hall. She peeked into her parents' bedroom, but they weren't there. Then she crept down the stairs. The house seemed deserted.

Where had everyone gone? Was this a nightmare? Was she the last person on Earth, and everyone else on the planet had been sucked up into the B-day Box?

Nadira spotted something in the living room that stopped her dead in her tracks. She put her hands over her mouth to cover the scream.

Standing against the fireplace was a brand new, solid red, extremely cool mountain bike!

"Happy Birthday!" cried Nadira's family as they jumped up from behind the couch.

"No way!" Nadira screamed, running over to the best birthday present ever! "A mountain bike? I've wanted one of these for forever!"

Nadira gave big hugs to everyone, even her brother. She was surprised to see that her grandparents were there, too. They had come into town extra early so they could be there when Nadira got her new bike. She gave them both extra hugs.

"We have one more present to give you before we sit down to breakfast," Grandma said, "and then all the rest will have to wait until the party this afternoon." She took Nadira by the hand. "Come with me."

Another present? What could it be? If it was worth her grandparents getting up early enough to drive into town for breakfast, then it must be something really special.

For the second time that morning, Nadira stopped dead in her tracks. She put her hand to her mouth, and this time she thought she really might scream. Her feet didn't seem to be touching the ground as the horrible smell of swimming pool chemicals filled her nose.

"Well," said Grandpa, "are you thrilled or are you thrilled?"

Nadira blinked and wanted to rub her eyes to make sure she wasn't imagining this. Her Grandma had once been a professional seamstress. Nadira had always been entranced by photos of the beautiful dresses she used to make for her customers. Her specialty was sewing traditional Indian wraps and saris. And now, right in front of Nadira, stood an old shop window display dummy wearing a lovely red and yellow sari.

Nadira recognized the sari—and the chemical smell. They were both from the 11th photograph!

"I . . . I . . . " Nadira stuttered. "I really don't know what to say."

"You don't have to say anything, dear," Grandma said, "just come try it on. I want to make sure it fits correctly."

Grandpa led Nadira over to the dummy. The chemical smell was almost too much to stand. Grandma noticed the face she was making and said, "That's just the smell of the yellow coloring chemical I had to use to dye the fabric. Don't worry, after I get this measured right, I'll run it through the washer."

Grandpa held up his ancient camera that looked like something out of a museum. "And then I can take a photo of you—you and everyone else, just like I do every year. It's tradition, you know."

Chapter 6
Grandma's Tale

Alexis came over just in time for lunch, and Nadira pulled her aside as soon as she walked in the door.

"Hey, birthday gi—Ow! You're hurting my arm."

"Alexis!" Nadira exclaimed, dragging her friend into the living room where they were out of earshot of the rest of the family. She tried to keep her anxious yelling down to a whisper-yell. "It's coming true!"

"What is?"

"The 11th photograph! My grandmother's made me a red sari—just like the one in the picture!"

"Wow. That's so cool." Then Alexis saw the expression on her friend's face, and quickly added, "OK, only a little bit cool."

"We have to make sure the other things in the picture don't come true," Nadira said.

"But how?"

"I don't know. We'll figure that out later. Let's start with my grandma."

Alexis nodded. "Maybe she knows something more about where the B-day Box came from."

After lunch the girls found Grandma sewing in the dining room. She was just finishing up the final seams on Nadira's new birthday sari. Nadira carried the B-day Box out in front of her like it was a piece of dynamite that might explode at any minute. She lightly set it on the table as she sat down. Alexis took the seat next to her.

"Hello there, Granddaughter," Grandma said. "Are you excited about your new sari? The pattern on this is very traditional. When I was a young girl growing up in India, I wasn't allowed to wear t-shirts and jeans like you and your brother. You're an American now, but it's also important for you to remember your cultural heritage and where you came from."

"Yes, Grandma, I will," Nadira answered, humbled by her grandmother's words. "I am very curious about India and where you grew up. That's why I wanted to ask about this box you bought for me." Nadira turned the box so her grandmother could see it better.

"Ah yes, your B-day Box," Grandma began as she threaded a new needle with red thread. "I bought that box from a merchant at the street market in Kolkata, one of the largest cities in India.

"The market is a very crowded and busy place. Vendors and merchants set up booths, tables, and baskets filled with anything and everything you might want to buy—fruits in all shapes and sizes, flowers of all the colors of the rainbow, warm blankets, hand-woven rugs, beautiful gold and silver jewelry, clothes in all sorts of styles, musical instruments, and anything else you can imagine can be found at the market.

"The narrow streets are filled with crowds of people looking for a bargain. They politely argue to see if the merchant will sell his merchandise for less money. And no one's better at getting a good price than your grandmother!"

Nadira smiled proudly. She was beginning to see that there was so much more to her grandmother than just clothes and sewing.

"On my last trip to Kolkata, I set aside one whole day to shop in the market. I had bought some fresh dates, which are my favorite fruit, and some fresh curry spice. Then it was time to find my granddaughter a nice present to bring home with me.

"I stopped at a wooden wagon stacked high with candles and perfumed oils, but neither was what I was looking for. Next to the wagon was a booth selling beautiful scarves, but that didn't seem right either.

"Just then, I heard a voice behind me say, 'You seek a special gift, am I right? Not a trinket or candle, but something special for a special . . . granddaughter?'

"I turned around and saw a very old man standing behind an empty table. He was mostly bald except for some long, white hair in the back, and he had deep wrinkles around his eyes. He actually took me quite by surprise, since I hadn't noticed him when I walked up. He might have appeared out of thin air for all I knew."

Nadira and Alexis both exchanged nervous glances.

"Well," Grandma continued, "there was nothing on the table, and I thought it was terribly strange for a merchant to be at the street market with nothing to sell, so I asked him, 'What do you sell, sir? Empty tables?'

"'I only sell one thing, Madam—the perfect gift for granddaughters,' he replied. Then he reached under his table and brought out a wooden box, the very box that's sitting on the table before us now," Grandma said, gesturing to the B-day Box.

"'How can you be certain that I'm shopping for my granddaughter?' I asked the old man.

"He just shrugged his shoulders and

said, 'You have the look of a caring grandmother.'

"Well, despite his strange behavior, the box was very beautiful, and as I looked it over, it did seem as though it'd be the perfect gift for you, Nadira. I'd seen the old shoebox you used to use for your B-day Box, and I thought this box would be perfect to replace it."

"So you bought the box from the strange old man?" Nadira asked.

"I did. We argued over the price for a minute—and you'll be happy to know that I got a very good deal on it—and I handed him the money. But before he handed me the box, he stopped.

"He looked at me very seriously for a moment, then he said, 'This box is for the girl, and no one else?'

"I nodded. Yes, it was to be a present for my granddaughter.

"The man smiled a little when I told him this. 'This box will be important to her. It will help her in a time of need. It will keep someone she cares about safe from danger.' And then he handed me the box."

Grandma stopped her story and looked over the sewing she'd done on the sari.

"Alright then, are you ready to get dressed?" Grandma asked, holding the sari out to Nadira.

"Wait. Get dressed?" Nadira exclaimed. "What about the old man? What about the market?"

"What do you mean?" Grandma looked confused. "I bought the box and brought it home to you. The end."

Nadira was about to fall out of her chair. What had the old man meant? Who was in danger? Danger from what?

Alexis also looked like she might fall out of her chair. "But what about the photograph?"

"Photograph? What photograph?" Grandma asked.

Nadira took the key from around her neck and unlocked the B-day Box. "I found something strange inside the box. Something that wasn't supposed to be there." Nadira opened the lid, then slid the box over to her grandmother.

Grandma stared into the box. "Yes? What is it?"

"What is it? It's a picture of—" Nadira turned the box back around and looked inside.

The 11th photograph was gone! It had appeared out of thin air, and it seemed to have disappeared into thin air as well.

Before Nadira was able to say anything more, Grandpa stuck his head into the dining room. "You ladies ready for the family picture?" he asked.

Chapter 7
The Horrible Event

With some help from her mother, Nadira switched into the red sari her grandmother had made for her. Sonali suggested adding a purple wrap for around her middle, to top things off. She also wanted Nadira to wear her hair down, which Grandma liked.

Nadira did as her mother suggested. She had no choice really. Although she wanted to do everything she could to make sure the things in the 11th photograph (wherever it was) never came true, she couldn't hurt her grandmother's feelings and not wear her new birthday present. After all, it really was a beautiful sari, and on any other day, it would have made Nadira feel wonderful.

Grandpa, who already had the family lined up in the correct positions in front of the fireplace for the annual picture, led the applause as Nadira entered the living room.

Wolfgang stood in his usual place as well, although his ears were drooping, and his head hung at a funny angle. Still,

Nadira was relieved to see that he was OK. The question was, for how long? She was certain that whenever her grandpa took the 11th photograph, that's when the horrible event would happen.

"Here she is," Grandpa smiled. "Is the birthday girl ready for the big shot?"

Nadira glanced around her, coming very close to panicking. She felt trapped. It was as though the walls might fall in on her. What was she going to do? Things were spinning out of control, and the 11th photograph was about to be taken!

She glanced over at Alexis, pleading with her eyes: *Do something*!

Alexis understood. She chewed her lip for a second as her mind raced to come up with a plan, then a bright smile spread across her face.

"I know! Would you guys mind if I joined the picture this year?"

The family stared at Alexis as though she were speaking a whole different language, but Nadira realized just what she was doing. A bright smile spread across her face as well.

The 11th photograph showed the Bakshi family standing in front of the fireplace with frightened looks on everyone's face. It also showed Nadira in her new red sari. But what the picture did not show was Alexis! If Alexis was in the picture, then the 11th photograph couldn't come true and the horrible event would be stopped!

"Yes! I'd love to have Alexis in my picture!" Nadira exclaimed.

Grandpa shrugged. "You're the birthday girl."

Alexis ran over and stood next to her friend, who finally breathed a sigh of relief. Things might actually turn out OK after all. Nadira put her arm around Alexis, then smiled for the camera—

And that's when she noticed that Wolfgang was missing.

"Wait!" Nadira cried. "Where's Wolfgang?"

"He just went out into the kitchen for a drink of water," Sonali said. "That dog is so thirsty lately. I don't know what's gotten into him. Would you go and fetch him please, Alexis?"

Alexis, who'd always seemed to be shy around Nadira's mother, immediately did as Sonali asked.

She was halfway across the room when Nadira screamed, "No, Alexis! Don't leave this room!"

But it was too late. Alexis was no longer in the camera shot, everyone had a grim, almost frightened look on their face, and Nadira herself looked as though she were screaming at something.

Then there was a click, followed by a blinding flash.

The 11ᵗʰ photograph had been taken.

The room was still and quiet. Nadira held her breath. The seconds stretched out, and still no one moved.

Finally Grandpa said with an embarassed smile, "Well, I'm sorry about

that, but when Nadira yelled at her friend, I was so startled that I pressed the camera shutter by mistake. And now I've completely run out of film."

"Can't we just make a run to the store, Dad?" Sonali asked.

"I'm afraid the camera shop where I get my film isn't open on weekends. I guess that's what I get for having such an old camera."

Nadira couldn't move. She stood stiff as a board, waiting to see what horrible thing had happened.

"You OK, Sis?" Naveen asked. "You look as pale as a sheet."

Tears of pure despair had sprung into Nadira's eyes, but even though the tears made everything look so blurry, she could still see that Wolfgang was nowhere to be found.

Then she heard Alexis's voice calling out from the kitchen, "Hey, you guys. I think you'd better come take a look at this."

Swallowing a tiny cry, Nadira was through the doorway like lightning, closely followed by her family.

"It's Wolfgang," Alexis said.

Nadira's dog was lying on his side next to his water dish, eyes barely open. His chest rose and fell rapidly with his shallow panting. It looked as though he'd collapsed while getting a drink. The water bowl was turned on its side, and water was splashed everywhere.

And because of this, Wolfgang's collar was soaking wet.

Chapter 8
Nadira's Worst Nightmare

Nadira and Alexis stayed behind as Anupam and Naveen rushed Wolfgang to the animal hospital. Anupam promised to call as soon as he knew anything. Until then, he told Nadira not to worry. Everything would be fine.

"Not much of a birthday is it?" Alexis asked. They sat out on the front steps, each with a piece of birthday cake, but neither really felt hungry.

"It's Wolfgang's birthday, too," Nadira responded. "It's not really much of a birthday for either of us."

"I'm sorry I ran out of the room," Alexis said. "I know I was supposed to be in the picture with you guys. If I had been, this might not have happened. It's all my fault."

"No, it's not," Nadira told her. "It's mine. The clues were all there, but I just wasn't able to put the pieces together. If I had, then we might have prevented this. This is my worst nightmare come true."

"What is?" asked a voice from behind them. It was Grandma, who came out onto the front porch and took a seat in a chair close by.

"Wolfgang's sick," Nadira replied, "and there must have been something I could have done, but—" She couldn't finish the thought.

"Nonsense!" Grandma protested. "Wolfgang's illness has nothing to do with you. The fact of the matter is that Wolfgang is not a young dog anymore. How old is he? Seven?"

"He's ten. Today's his birthday, too."

Grandma smiled warmly. "Ten may be young for humans, but it's old for dogs. And you've taken good care of him. You feed him well and take him on walks. He still has a long life ahead of him.

"Someday, the family photo won't have absolutely everyone in it. Wolfgang won't always be with us, but that's nothing to be afraid of. What's important is that you always treasure the memories of the time that you do have with Wolfgang."

Nadira was silent. Now she really didn't want any birthday cake.

"That's why I'm glad to see that you still keep your B-day Box," Grandma continued. "It's important to keep old photos and keepsakes so that you'll be able to remember all of your good birthdays."

"My B-day Box isn't really giving me many good memories at the moment," Nadira said.

"Why not?"

Nadira shot a look at Alexis, who nodded her head. "Tell her."

"I found a strange photo in with all my other birthday pictures," Nadira began. "I found it two nights ago, but it was a picture of today! It was the photo Grandpa took. I knew all about the red sari, and the smell of the yellow dye, and Wolfgang's collar."

Grandma reached a hand out and brushed Nadira's hair out of her face. "Don't be so hard on yourself, Granddaughter."

Nadira was quiet, though she was grateful for her grandmother's kind words.

"You know," Grandma said, "the man who sold me that box told me that it would help you in a time of need. And I think it has."

"Helped? How? Wolfgang's still sick. I didn't help him at all!"

"Yes, you did," Grandma said. "No one else in the family noticed anything strange about Wolfgang, but you did. You noticed that he's been acting unusual. You insisted that your father drive him to the animal hospital, even on a Sunday!

"Whatever it was that you found in that box, it made you pay closer attention to Wolfgang. Dogs sleep a lot. Dogs drink a lot of water. So what? But you knew that something was really wrong. Otherwise, it might have been another week or more before we decided to get him checked out. Things might have been a lot worse by then."

Grandma's words made some sense, and without really meaning to, Nadira started to feel better.

Just then, the front door swung open. Sonali stood there with the phone to her ear.

"It's your father," she said. "Wolfgang's going to be OK!"

Chapter 9
The B-day Box

The very next weekend, Nadira sat on the floor of the living room in her pajamas, surrounded by a mountain of blankets. Alexis was laid out on the floor next to her, fast asleep. The TV was on, providing the only light in the room. Nadira wondered if, after everything she'd been through, the spooky shadows on the walls would scare her—but she sort of enjoyed them.

The rest of the house was quiet, and Nadira had promised her brother Naveen that if he tried to scare them again, she'd be ready. She had a cold glass of ice water ready to splash him if she heard him coming down the stairs.

Nadira and Alexis were having another sleepover with lots of movies, popcorn, and laughing, only this time there were no promises to stay up until midnight. At half past ten, Alexis was already snoring.

Wolfgang was also fast asleep. Nadira had moved his bed right beside her, so she could reach over and scratch behind his ears. She stroked his head, and Wolfgang opened his eyes, panted, and licked her hand. She leaned in so she could get doggie kisses on her face, which Wolfgang was happy to give.

Nadira had been terribly frightened when her father had returned from the animal hospital last weekend without Wolfgang. Anupam explained that he'd had to leave Wolfgang with the doctors overnight so they could watch him and make sure he got what he needed. There was nothing for her to worry about, although Nadira still worried anyway.

The veterinarian said that Wolfgang had a mild case of canine diabetes, which is very similar to human diabetes. It's a disease in the blood where the body is not able to produce enough of a chemical it needs called insulin. The blood uses insulin to process the sugar we eat into something the body can use. Not having enough insulin in the blood to process sugar can be very dangerous.

Dogs who have diabetes will sleep and drink much more than usual. Anupam told Nadira that she'd been right to worry when she noticed that Wolfgang was acting strangely. If she had not told him what she'd seen, he might never have taken Wolfgang to the vet. He might have thought that Wolfgang was just extra tired. Nadira felt good about that. She thought that maybe she'd helped Wolfgang out after all.

The good news was that they'd caught Wolfgang's diabetes early. He'd stayed at the animal hospital for a few days. Now that they had him home, they watched his diet closely and gave him plenty of exercise, and Nadira's mother gave him a small shot of insulin every morning. Wolfgang was going to be OK.

Nadira chuckled at Alexis's snoring. She was very grateful for her friend's help, even if she never would be able to stay up until midnight with her.

She held the real-life 11th photograph in her hand. She smiled at it now, despite all the trouble it had caused. Her mouth was wide open in the picture as she screamed at Alexis, telling her not to leave the room. It actually looked pretty funny.

Grandpa had offered to retake the picture after he'd bought more film for his old camera, but Nadira said no. This picture would be fine. It would be a reminder of all that she'd gone through. It captured everything that had happened on her 11th birthday. And those memories, even though they weren't all good, weren't all bad either. They were worth saving.

Nadira pulled her B-day Box out from under the blankets. She would keep this 11th photograph with all the rest.

She took the small, metal key from around her neck, and with a slight click, she unlocked the box and lifted the lid.

As she put the 11th photograph inside the box, she noticed something strange. She saw something else, something new and frightening in the B-day Box that wasn't supposed to be there . . .